The CRATE Way

The CRATE Way

The Homeowner's Step-by-Step Guide
to a Painless Remodel

Scott Monday

Published by kitchen & bath CRATE
info@kbcrate.com
Modesto, CA

Cover Design by Michaela McDermott

Book Design by Kory Kirby
SET IN MINION PRO

ISBN 978-1-7372923-0-2 (paperback)
ISBN 978-1-7372923-1-9 (eBook)

Printed in the United States of America

Contents

Welcome to the CRATE Way

I Want You to Achieve Your Remodel Goals

The dread. You have a renovation project coming up, and you know it needs to get done. You have a general sense of what you want the project to look like—and maybe a hint of how to actually pull it off—but still you dread it. You're not certain where to begin or what steps to take along the way. And this uncertainty is the reason, five years later, that the project has yet to start.

This is an all-too-common scenario customers share with us at kitchen & bath CRATE, the company I started back in 2012 with the sole intent of "changing the way customers perceive our industry." And if *we* hear this on a regular basis from those we serve in a tiny sliver of the United States, then there have to be tens of thousands around the nation in this same quandary.

So that's why I wrote this book for you. In it I'll cover the remodeling process from start to finish, culling information from my more than twenty years of construction experience and my favorite online resources. I'll even pull the curtain back and show you actual documents we use with our customers.

Allow Me to Be Your Copilot on This Journey

When our team meets with clients considering a remodel, they often tell us they have no idea where to start. We use the same steps in this book to guide them through their remodel project, and we assure you these steps are "real-world" proven.

But you may be asking, *Since this information is coming from a contractor, won't it be skewed in favor of contractors, excusing their behavior and justifying their weaknesses?*

Actually, it won't be.

Here's why: We know our industry is broken. We know that contractors have a well-deserved reputation of dismissing deadlines, being rude during customer service, and, at their worst, conducting business in a questionable or unethical way. And that's exactly why we came up with a different way: the CRATE Way.

What Is the "CRATE Way"?

You may be wondering about this whole "CRATE Way" thing.

It started at Costco, of all places. My wife and I had just checked out and were walking down the exit aisle. You know the one: the aisle where they sell tires and cars and pergolas and all those other big-ticket items. I can't recall which of us asked the question, but one of us looked at the other and said, "Why can't you buy your kitchen remodel and have it arrive in a huge box?"

As absurd as the question was, my wife and I started riffing on the concept in a half-joking manner. "Why couldn't you design your remodel in the store, at a kiosk, then have someone come out and measure your home and make sure it would all fit? Then why couldn't they load all the materials in a huge box and deliver it with a helicopter to the front of your house?"

On and on we went, our ideas becoming more absurd . . .

Or were they?

Despite the implausibility of helicopter delivery and such, there *was* something to this idea. After all, the industry was rife with pain points (check out our "Avoiding the Pain" tips and tricks highlighted throughout this book), and the world of remodeling was ready for disruption.

So we came up with a pain-solving concept we call the "CRATE Way."

- Customers want to be fully confident their jobs wrap up on time, so we offer a $250-per-day guarantee that we'll finish on the day we promised.
- Customers want a turnkey solution, so we offer estimates, design, permits, construction, and warranty for one set price.
- Customers want peace of mind even after their project ends, so we offer a two-year complete project warranty, double the length offered by most of our competitors.
- Customers want expert guidance when choosing materials and fixtures, so every project comes with interior design services from certified designers.
- Customers want a clear understanding of their project costs, so we offer line-by-line project breakdowns for their approval long before jobs begin.
- Customers want the cleanest possible home during their renovation, so we use the CRATE (an 8' x 16' repurposed storage container that acts as a jobsite hub) and a rigorous daily cleanup process to ensure we're keeping things neat and tidy during the remodel.

- Customers don't want shady strangers in their home, so we use only in-house team members or a handful of heavily screened subcontractors to perform the work.

And you know what? It worked!

In year one we completed a whopping three kitchen & bath CRATE projects. The next year: twenty-seven. Then sixty-eight. Then 107. Now we complete well over two hundred remodels a year.

The secret is simple: By using the CRATE Way, keeping our promises, and treating customers the way we want to be treated, we started to change the perception of our industry, one homeowner at a time.

Now part of my mission is to share the CRATE Way. By doing so, customers will hold my industry to a higher standard, expect more, and receive better service. It's important to me. I want my kids and grandkids to be proud of our family company and the industry we work in.

So let's dive right in and start your journey to a painless kitchen or bathroom remodel via the CRATE Way!

—*Scott Monday,* founder, kitchen & bath CRATE,
March 2021, Modesto, California

DEFINING YOUR REMODEL:

From Idea to Action

Our Dirty Little Secret

People don't believe us when we tell them this, but here's a little contractor secret.

You ready?

Here goes: *The hardest part of any construction project happens BEFORE work even starts.*

That's right. All the little parts and pieces that have to be attended to before work begins are by far the most time-consuming, stressful, and important facets of a painless remodel. (We're assuming, of course, that you don't jump in to your remodel without thought. This would, of course, minimize the "planning" stage but surely ruin the "execution" stage.)

How can this be, you ask?

The main challenge is getting your idea from your head into your contractor's head. Since we lack telepathic ability, there has to be a process to ensure your builder knows what you want. If not, you'll encounter issue after issue during and after construction.

The key elements of defining your project are:

- beginning with the end in mind
- harnessing the power of visual inspiration
- translating your idea to "contractor-speak"

Let's look a bit deeper at these three elements.

Begin with the End in Mind (Let's Get Zen)

OK, do this: Pull out a blank piece of paper and grab a pencil (not a pen).

Sit down at a desk or table and remove yourself from the chaos of your day for just a minute. Place the paper in front of you. Grab the pencil. Close your eyes (not while you're reading this, of course, but you get the idea).

Now finish these five sentences:

- When I walk into my newly remodeled space, I want to see . . .
- When people see my new remodel, I want them to think . . .
- The three things I most want to see changed about my space are . . .
- If I had to choose between high quality and low cost, I would choose . . .
- My budget for my remodel is around . . .

This visualization phase brings to mind a pair of recent clients. Let's call them Samantha and Pete. While working with them through their kitchen design, it became apparent that their weekly dinners with their extended family were the highlight of their week. So while they wanted a kitchen that worked for day-to-day use, they *really* wanted a kitchen that accommodated their family gatherings.

Our design team put our heads together and came up with perhaps the largest, most impressive, most useful island I've ever seen. Imagine a bar top, food-preparation station, and dining table all rolled into one central island feature.

Samantha and Pete reported back a few weeks after construction ended: "Scott, we had our first massive family dinner last night, and I can't tell you how well our island-table thing worked. It is perfect and made these events, which were already special, that much better."

A true testament to the importance of thinking through your project vision before you do anything else, right?

OK, so now that you've completed the five sentences above, you are now officially further along your remodel than many people ever get. You've visualized your remodel, you've identified what you want others to think, you've identified the major pain points that are causing the remodel, and you've declared a distinct financial direction for the project.

Good job! Now go have a glass of wine to celebrate. Or go to the next item . . .

AVOIDING THE PAIN:
All Alone in Planning Your Project?

When my first child was born in 2006, there were a lot of things running through my head. Perhaps you felt the same with your first child, first job, or first relocation to a new town.

I can sum it up like this: I had no idea what I was doing. (If I'm being honest, I sometimes still feel this way!)

In fact, I didn't even know what I didn't know, and when I

did find out that I needed something or had to do something, I then had to figure out how to do it or where to get it. Then, only then, did I realize that what I got, or what I was doing, was probably not right, and it was back to square one. It was like that iconic scene in *I Love Lucy* where Lucy and Ethel are shoving chocolates into their mouths as the conveyor belt increases speed.

These memories remind me of stories I've heard from customers when they describe their previous remodel experiences with the "other guys."

You see, it's common for the "other guys" to provide a bid (if you can even call it that) and then look you straight in the eye and say, "Well, let me know when you have all your stuff picked out."

What? How is that even possible? How can this "professional," who's been doing this for DECADES, ask his customers to "pick everything out"? How does the customer even know what they need? How does the contractor know the customer will get all the correct materials, fixtures, and components?

This is precisely why your remodeler should not only include interior design on each project but also create a multipage project data sheet, down to the smallest detail, after the design meeting concludes.

Based on their feedback, customers love it. The design phase is an interactive, educational, and even enjoyable process. What's more exciting than leaning on experts whose sole role is to translate your dream project into real-life selections and specifications? You get to do the fun part while your contractor does the heavy lifting.

After all, isn't that what you're looking for?

Harnessing the Power of Visual Inspiration

Now some fun stuff.

We live in an age of unprecedented visual inspiration. We have endless access to the wonderful things other people have created, and we have splendid tools with which to organize them. Instagram, Houzz, and Pinterest are full of millions of inspiring photos. YouTube and HGTV have brought us more remodel, flipping, and real estate video footage than we could watch in a lifetime. And our friends and family share their remodel projects on social media right and left.

So now it's time for you to go on a picture-hunting expedition. You can use whatever form of medium you like: social media apps, the internet, books, magazines, and the homes of friends and family. All are perfectly acceptable options.

No matter which medium you choose, start gathering images and saving them in an online database or on your phone, tablet, or computer. You can print or copy them and place them in a file folder. Your goal is to gather images and ideas—inspiration, if you will. There's no wrong medium here. Any form of inspiration will help.

Here's what that might look like if you're a bit more technically inclined:

Let's say you need a kitchen remodel. When completing our little zen exercise above, you landed on quartzite countertops, two-tone frameless cabinets, a contemporary tile backsplash, modern plumbing fixtures, and top-of-the-line appliances.

OK, perfect. Now visit a great image site for homes (Houzz, Instagram, and Pinterest are good options). Search for kitchens and take a look around. Every time you get that "I love it!" feeling about a picture, capture it by saving it within the website/app you're using or in a separate folder on your device or computer. The tool you use to store and capture images isn't the important thing, so long as you can easily access the images later.

Do this for a few minutes each day, and in no time you'll have a significant visual library to inspire your project.

Translating Your Idea to Contractor-Speak

All right, you're making great progress, and all in one short afternoon. You've established guiding principles for your remodel, you've collected a lot of inspiration, and now it's time to translate that into contractor-speak.

But to do that, you need to know how contractors think. Bear in mind, most contractors (the good ones, at least) are highly analytical. They're not the touchy-feely, "let's sit down and have a deep conversation" types. They succeed or fail based on fact, reduction of risk, and financial responsibility. Of course, a good contractor wants you to have exactly what you want. But they also want enough clarity to accurately implement your job and satisfy you.

You have two choices for translating the job from your head to contractor-speak:

- Hire an interior designer, architect, or design-build contractor to produce this translation.
- Write a scope of work for your contractor.

Each method has its strengths and weaknesses. The former requires you to pay for services (unless you use kitchen & bath CRATE or a similar design-build contractor) but will provide you with a set of plans. The latter just costs you time, but it does require a working knowledge of materials and methods. We'll talk more about designers in "Designing and Specifying," so for now let's look at the self-performing method.

A scope of work is simply a bullet-point list of what you want. Here's an example:

Scope of Work
Project: Sample Project
Location: Sample Address, City, State, Zip

- **Hall Bathroom**
  - Demo existing bath and fixtures.
  - Rough-in for new shower.
  - Supply & install new shower pan specification KOYA with drain on right and seat on left in white (Abe's)
  - Repair/replace drywall with green board as needed.
  - Supply & install new prefabricated surround by BCI, available from Cal Bath specification Marble Finish Travertine Simulated 12 x 12 Slate on square.
    - ◆ Add 4-Shelf Rectangular Corner Caddy Biscuit Color located in back right of shower.
    - ◆ One 16" grab bar color Biscuit installed at Owner's specified location.
  - Supply & install new shower head/mixing valve full-height Kingsley Envi Three-Function Eco-Performance Showerhead 3233EP+.
  - Supply & install new removable shower head/mixing valve sitting-height Kingsley Four-Function with wall bracket 3836. (Hose to be 59" not standard 69").
  - Supply & install new S-curve shower doors specification SE-2000C – S Curve 58" 70-3/4" Chrome Trim on all surfaces other than frame which should be brushed nickel. (Adam @ Don's)
  - Replace sheet vinyl with new sheet vinyl Congoleum "Creamy Beige" 179057
    - ◆ NO SEAM!
  - Install new humidity sensor, no light exhaust fan by Owner.
  - Install new Kohler toilet by Owner.
- **Master Bathroom**
  - Demo drywall bedroom side to access mixing valve.
  - Demo existing soap holder and supply & install new brushed nickel soap holder.

- Retrofit new mixing valve with oversized base plate specification Kingsley Posi-Temp Mixing Valve T2112NH, and Moen 1920BN Remodeling Cover Plate For Two and Three Handle Tub/Showers In Brushed Nickel
- Supply & install new shower head specification Kingsley Envi Three-Function Eco-Performance Showerhead 3233EP+.
- Patch drywall bedroom side.
- Install new humidity sensor, with light exhaust fan by Owner.
  - Fan shall be on timer and light in fan on switch. Owner to be sure fan they purchase has this functionality.
- Refinish sink countertop and window sill to like-new condition. No work at cabinet.
- Existing sink to remain.
- Supply & install new faucet specification Kingsley 6102 brushed nickel with deck plate.
- Install new toilet by Owner specification Toto Ultra-Max order from Abe's as per Abe's estimate and spec sheet.
- Replace sheet vinyl with new sheet vinyl specification Congoleum "Creamy Beige" 179057
  - NO SEAM! (Use vinyl remaining after hall bath floor install)
- Supply & install new shower door specification P-2000 – 24" x 66-5/8" with Rain Glass and brushed nickel trim. (Don's)

- **Living Room**
  - Supply & install new pocket door from kitchen to living room to match existing.
  - Drywall patch as needed.
  - Replace slider with new slider 8068 Anderson to match

Family Room slider with screen; hardware Newbury Antique Brass.

- ◆ Cal Comfort – Confirm door handle style options with Andy
- ▫ Re-frame for new bay window Pella 45 degree bay 95" x 59" casement operators with slim shades, aluminum-clad exterior, primed interior with head and seat boards.
  - ◆ Cal Comfort – Confirm color with Andy
- ▫ Patch drywall at bay window as needed.
- ▫ Patch plaster at bay window as needed.
- ▫ Install two 4" dimmable mini-cans above new bay window specification...

- ■ **Family Room**
  - ▫ Repair rough opening at slider to improve sliding action – Discuss with Andy.
  - ▫ Install new pendant lighting over extended countertop specification...
    - ◆ Owner will supply pendant lighting from Phillips Electric, and will mark ceiling location with painter's tape for installation. Fixture should be centered above width of countertop extension, roughly where the long tape mark on the temporary top is located. Fixture base will be closer to first beam than to wall above upper cabinets.
  - ▫ Install new dimmable track lighting in family room specification...
    - ◆ Owner will supply track lighting and dimmer from Phillips Electric, and will mark ceiling locations with painter's tape for installation. Burt placed blue tape on the beams where the track lighting will be located—on beam on either side of fireplace, on beam on patio side and above chairs/desk top, and

on beam on patio side above audio cabinet (tape is
on wall with notation pointing to beam)

◻ Repair wiring short at fan.

- **Guest Bedroom**

  ◻ Remove and dispose of area rug.

- **Master Bedroom**

  ◻ Remove and dispose of existing carpet.

- **Kitchen**

  ◻ Demo and re-frame kitchen window to lower sill height
  while maintaining a 4" backsplash with rounded top
  edge.

    ◆ Casement window need only open on left side when
    facing out.

  ◻ Demo countertops.

  ◻ Supply & install new cabinet bay as per revised mock-up.

    ◆ Must include trash pull-out drawer specification...

  ◻ Stain and finish new cabinet to match existing as close
  as possible.

  ◻ Supply & install new sink Kohler Brookfield Under-
  mount Biscuit (K5942-5U-96) with Duo Drain disposal
  flange in stainless steel (Abe's)

  ◻ Supply & install soap dispenser as per Abe's specification.

  ◻ Supply cutting board as per Abe's specification.

  ◻ Supply & install new countertops Silestone Capri Limestone full bullnose with rounded edges at sink and zero
  reveal; seam to be on entry hall side of countertop.
  Extend countertop to total length of 181" (56" beyond
  existing tile countertop); 33-35" widest in new portion
  (template to be made).

  ◻ Supply and install 4" Silestone Capri Limestone backsplash with rounded top edge along sink side walls.

  ◻ Supply and install Silestone Capri Limestone on stove
  side to replace full height of current tile wall covering.

- Supply & install new faucet Price Pfister Parisa 534 series Pull-out Spray polished chrome (Abe's)
- Install new garbage disposal specification...
- Install under-cabinet LED dimmable lighting specification...
- Install 5" can lights in kitchen quantity and specification...
  - Owner marked ceiling locations with painter's tape for installation. Note: Owner marked five rough locations, but are open to suggestion as to whether six are preferable to five, and to adjustment of locations
- Supply & install new cased opening from hall entry to kitchen.

- **Exterior**
  - Replace all windows specification fiberglass double pane casement (other than bay) paintable both sides.
  - Supply & install new gutters on all hip roofs standard 7" fascia gutter.
  - Remove and replace flat roof over Burt's desk with new insulated flat roof.
    - Owner to treat for pests during this time.
  - Paint exterior specification...
  - Add two new outlets on outside of home.
- **Interior**
  - Refinish ALL wood floors, including Master Bedroom, Guest Bedroom, Office, hallway and entryway (to natural red oak, as current)
  - Supply & install new red oak hardwood flooring in kitchen and family room to match existing.
    - Supply & install custom medallion at fireplace after owner alters fireplace hearth. (A Step Above)
  - Stain and finish new wood flooring to match existing natural red oak.

- ▫ Paint interior ceilings, hall walls and cabinets.
  - ◆ Owner will designate color
- ▫ Paint hall bath cabinets.
  - ◆ Color as per existing shade of white
- ▫ Add CO_2 detector at hallway.
- ▫ Supply & install new door at furnace closet to match existing.
- ▫ Add recirculating pump on hot water heater.
- ▪ **Attic**
  - ▫ Refurbish or replace existing attic fan (automatic thermostat on unit)

It can be arranged by room, area of room (floor, walls, ceilings), or trade (flooring, plumbing, electrical, tile, cabinets). Either way, it's a thorough listing of what you want (or what you think you might want).

To help create such a scope, here is a list of standard elements of a residential remodel. Take it one step at a time, filling it in as you go. Before you know it, you'll have a completed scope of work.

Standard Elements of a Residential Remodel			
		ITEM	NOTES
Soft Costs			
	2	Building Permit	
	3	Misc. Rental Equipment	
	4	Debris Boxes	
	5	Landfill Fees	
Demolition and Abatement			
	7	Building Demolition	
	8	Concrete Sawing	
	9	Asbestos Testing	
	10	Asbestos Removal	

		ITEM	NOTES
	Concrete		
12		Building Concrete	
13		Spoil Removal	
14		Trench Patching	
	Decorative Partitions		
16		Glass Block	
	Metals		
18		Stainless Steel	
19		Kitchen Hoods	
20		Ornamental Metals	
	Carpentry		
22		General Cleanup Labor	
23		Rough Carpentry Labor	
24		Rough Carpentry Material	
25		Rough Carpentry Hardware	
26		Finish Carpentry Labor	
27		Wood Baseboard	
28		Finish Carpentry Material	
29		Install Owner Items	
	Cabinets and Countertops		
31		Cabinets	
32		Ceramic Tile Countertops	
33		Natural Stone Countertops	
34		Engineered Stone Countertops	
35		Plastic Laminate Tops	
36		Stainless Steel Countertops	

		ITEM	NOTES
Thermal and Moisture Protection			
38		Thermal Insulation	
39		Roofing	
40		Caulking and Sealants	
Doors and Windows			
42		Door/Frames/Hardware Material	
43		Doors/Frames/ Hardware Labor	
44		Glass and Glazing	
45		Nail-on Windows	
Wall Finishes			
47		Drywall	
48		Metal Wall Finishes	
49		Wall Covering	
50		Wall Covering Labor	
51		Painting	
Floor Finishes			
53		Ceramic Tile	
54		Natural Stone Tile	
55		Wood Flooring	
56		Resilient Flooring (Sheet Vinyl or VCT)	
57		Wood Baseboard	
Appliances			
59		Refrigerator	
60		Range	
61		Microwave	
62		Dishwasher	
63		Ice Maker	
64		Wine Refrigerator	
65		Trash Compactor	

		ITEM	NOTES
Decoration			
67		Blinds and Shades	
68		Misc. Décor	
Systems			
70		Plumbing	
71		Heating and Air Conditioning	
72		Electrical	

■ ■ ■

Chapter Recap

- The hardest part of any construction project happens BEFORE work even starts.
- Begin with the end in mind.
- Harness the power of visual inspiration.
- Translate your idea to contractor-speak.

Deciding if You Are Ready for a Remodel

Are You Ready to Remodel?

Now that you've properly defined your remodel project, momentum is on your side.

If you followed our simple instructions, you have a firm grasp of your project goals, you've committed your project requirements to paper, you've collected assorted inspiration for your project, and you've translated your project to contractor-speak.

So what's next, you ask?

Deciding if you want to actually *do* the project is a good place to go from here.

In this chapter we'll deal with two critical elements in deciding if you want to proceed with your project: money and time.

Concept Budgeting

Concept budgeting is simply a rough estimate of your project budget based on your known scope of work to date. Is that too technical? Try this: A concept budget is an educated guess of project costs.

There are a few ways you can get a concept budget for your project.

Soliciting Concept Budgets from Contractors

Hands down, this method gets you the most accurate budget possible. It also requires early discussions with a general contractor.

For example, at kitchen & bath CRATE, we offer free phone consultations to all potential customers. (We also offer free in-home consultations and proposals, but that comes later.) During this call a CRATE team member assesses the scope of work and then offers a concept budget for the project. All this usually takes thirty minutes or less.

To some, this is too early in the process to actually work with a builder. But remember that most reputable contractors will work with you at this stage at no charge, hoping to impress you with their thoroughness and communication skills, thus gaining your trust for the construction phase of the project.

Other contractors would rather just wait until you're sure of the project and have complete plans and specifications for bidding. To each their own. Your best bet, should you use this method, is to openly and honestly tell your contractor where you are in the process. Then let them decide if they have the time and resources to help.

Note of Extreme Importance: Do NOT under any circumstance get multiple bids in this phase of the project. It's a waste of your time and certainly your contractor's time. There is no accurate way for contractors to bid a project at this phase, and you'll be making your decision based on inaccurate and incomparable information.

At kitchen & bath CRATE we respectfully decline any such requests to bid a project at this stage.

Building Your Own Spreadsheet

Perhaps you have some remodel experience and some spreadsheet knowledge, and you want to assemble a project budget yourself. Good for you! Nothing wrong with that. Here's an approach you may consider:

1. Download a simple budget worksheet at: *kbcrate.com/downloads* or make your own spreadsheet based on this example.
2. Using the scope of work you created earlier, input your best guess of costs for each project element. If an element is not applicable to your project, leave it blank.
3. If you encounter a row in the budget that you are unsure of, call a local vendor in that trade and chat with them about potential costs. They'll usually give you a ballpark figure right over the phone.
4. You're done! The number at the bottom of the spreadsheet will be a great approximation of your project cost.

Using Online Calculators

The internet has many online cost calculators. Some are better than others.

The main drawback with online calculators is they use general, lump-sum calculations instead of the more accurate line-by-line method used in the steps above. Nevertheless, they are often a good starting point. Here are a few links:

- *kbcrate.com/calculator*
- *homeadvisor.com/cost*
- *remodelingcalculator.org*

Now that you're armed with a concept budget for your project, consider the specific timing of your potential remodel.

Timing Factors to Consider with Your Remodel

Project Duration

Consider how long your project might take. Project duration ranges from a few weeks for a simple kitchen or bathroom remodel to a few months for a major down-to-the-studs renovation. If there are structural modifications involved, add even more time to the equation.

To minimize project duration, do the following before starting work:

- Secure building permits, if required.
- Select your finishes.
- Inquire on material "lead time" for your selections. "Lead time" is the number of days from when a product is ordered until it arrives on-site.
- Sign contracts with your contractors. Reviewing contracts can take a while, and doing this before work starts not only protects you but allows you to edit the contract to meet your needs without the pressure of construction being underway.

Major Life Events

Now that you have an approximate project duration, go through your calendar and see what major life events may interfere. Do you have a significant family event on the horizon, especially one you must host? Are there any imminent marriages or births?

If so, be sure you honestly assess each of these events and how they may cause you added stress. Remodeling can be stressful without other contributing factors.

Let me give you an example. A number of years ago we had a customer with a project just about to begin. The project schedule was approved, the CRATE was placed, and the temporary toilet was on-site. Then we got a call: "Scott, we can't start tomorrow! I just realized we have [a high-ranking official in their Catholic church] staying with us, and there is no way we can have his bathroom under construction!"

So what did we do? We made way for the pope! We removed the CRATE and the temporary toilet, and we rewrote the schedule and adjusted the project timeline. But I tell you, it was painful for all involved. Best to foresee such time conflicts early in the process, as you now know.

Holidays

Remodeling around holidays, especially between Thanksgiving and New Year's Day, can be challenging for a homeowner. Once again, honestly assess your responsibilities during these times and ensure they mesh with your remodel.

You can always elect to take a break from remodeling during holidays, but in our experience, a project sitting without being worked on is as stressful as work taking place.

Conversely, many contractors slow in the winter months, so intentionally scheduling your project for this time may lead to cost savings from your contractor.

Seasons

If your remodel involves roofing, windows, or exterior work in general, think through the approaching seasons. Any good contractor can handle weather issues that arise in wet months, but weather will delay the project and could add to the stress of the remodel (not to mention that an unusually wet winter could cause significant project delays).

Even if your project is entirely indoors, rain and snow will cause more dirt and mud to be tracked into your home than during dry months. Be sure to address this issue with your contractor up front, and establish expectations for flooring protection, access to the home, and cleanup standards.

Conclusion

You've now thoroughly considered both the money and time aspects of your project. It's time to make a decision: Do you want to proceed?

If not, table your project for a while. Perhaps circumstances will change and you'll be ready in a few months. But if you're ready to rock and roll, it's time to consider your permitting approach for the project.

■ ■ ■

Chapter Recap

- Consider money and time when deciding whether to go ahead with a project.
- Develop a concept budget by soliciting one from contractors or building your own spreadsheet.
- Consider timing factors such as project duration, major life events, holidays, and seasons.

Dealing with Building Departments

Now that you've defined your remodel and decided to move forward, the detailed planning can begin. Next up: permitting.

Why is permitting important? Your permitting strategy determines which design professionals you need to partner with and also significantly impacts your project schedule. Add permitting to the very long list of things many folks wait too long to address, costing time and money.

Permitting Is Confusing—Let's Simplify It

Permitting is basically getting your project certified, or approved, by your local building department. There are hundreds of different types of permits, and each and every jurisdiction (for example, county or city) approaches permitting differently.

Since this book focuses on kitchen and bathroom remodels, you're really dealing with one type of permitting: building permits. (Planning permits are typically triggered by changes to exterior features such as additions, expansions, and fencing installations.)

Basic building permits require submittal of a permit application with either plans or a description of work. The building department then reviews the application, asks for clarifications as needed, and issues the building permit. At this point, it's up to the homeowner (or contractor) to obtain inspections throughout the construction process. Your building official will advise which inspections are required. Upon job completion, a final inspection is conducted. When this inspection is passed, your project is complete in the eyes of the building department.

Do I Need a Permit?

Here's a good rule of thumb: You need a permit if you need an inspection.

What kinds of activities typically require an inspection?

- Anything that affects the structure of the building
- Plumbing
- Electrical
- Framing
- Concrete
- Masonry other than decorative veneer
- Insulation
- Roofing
- Drywall
- Pools or spas
- Fencing over 6' (typically)
- Closing off exterior doors or windows

Of course, when you secure a permit, you need an inspection. And this reminds me of one of my favorite inspection stories.

When we build a new shower, we waterproof the shower walls and floor in an assortment of ways, including what's called a "pan liner." A pan liner is a dense rubber membrane fused at the corners. It's placed under the tile mortar bed as a last line of defense against water infiltration.

One inspection the building departments conduct (at least in California) is a "pan liner inspection." This inspection requires the pan liner to be set, the drain to be plugged, and the pan liner to be filled to the top with water (we mark the waterline with a permanent marker as a reference point). After twenty-four hours the water still needs to be at the marker line. If so, the inspector passes the pan liner inspection, and we can carry on with tile.

We had one project where we could not get the water to stay at the line. We failed the inspection two or three times before realizing the homeowner's dog was drinking out of the shower pan all night. And this was a big dog. (Perhaps a descendant of a camel?) It drank so much water that the inspector thought there surely was a leak!

Long story short, the homeowner figured this out when they heard the dog slurping up the "inspection water" one night, and we all had a good laugh. (Except our project manager, who had to get the job back on schedule after the delay . . .)

So How Do I Get a Permit?

Depending on the extent of your project, you might be able to get by with a description of work instead of a full set of plans. Check with your building department on this issue. (To illustrate the wide range of permitting requirements, kitchen & bath CRATE has been required to provide as little as a five-word description of work all the way to fully dimensioned construction plans, all for the exact SAME project scope. Hard to believe, right?)

If plans are required, you'll need to hire an interior designer, architect, design-build contractor, and possibly an engineer. To find a local architect, check with the American Institute of Architects (AIA) by using their architect-finder tool: *aia.org/resources/6155589-find-an-architect*. The AIA is a long-established professional organization for architects and designers. It's a great starting point.

Once you find your designer, the next step is agreeing on a price and then moving forward with the design. This is money well spent. Not only will you ensure your project meets proper code requirements, but architects will bring a wealth of project experience, often quickly solving design challenges that have stumped homeowners for years.

Warning: Bypassing the Permitting Process

As you can tell by the information above, your project may not require a permit if it pertains solely to cosmetic, nonstructural improvements. If that's the case, you've saved yourself quite a bit of effort and money. Good for you!

If you decide to forgo the permitting process *despite knowing you need one*, be prepared for the following outcomes:

- Inability to sell your home due to noncompliant construction. This is often flagged by the inspectors during the transaction, and many lenders will subsequently not lend.
- Risk of the improvements causing injury or death. If your nonpermitted carport falls during a wild graduation party, you will be on the hook, and your insurance company may not offer much support. Quite a tragedy on many levels.

The cost and time saved by not permitting your project is rarely worth the risk.

■ ■ ■

Chapter Recap

- Your permitting strategy determines which design professionals you need to partner with and also significantly impacts your project schedule.
- You need a permit if you need an inspection.
- Determine whether you need a description of work or a full set of plans.
- Know the risks of forgoing the permitting process.

The Importance of the Details

Now that you've defined your remodel, decided to move forward, and dealt with any permitting issues, we can move on to designing and specifying your project.

Designing and specifying your project can take one of two distinct routes: creating a detailed scope document or generating a set of plans.

The Scope Document Method

In the first chapter, we discussed specifying your project using a scope of work document. For small projects or for homeowners with extensive remodeling experience, this could be all that's needed.

If that's the case, go back to your scope document (hopefully it's on your computer and neatly filed away, ready for edits!) and review it for accuracy. If you haven't done so already, take a few field trips to local stores and suppliers and start getting into the details. For example, instead of identifying "wood baseboard" for a room, specify "5½" MDF Coronado baseboard, painted."

Evaluate your project piece by piece, and define it well. This allows you to solicit more accurate pricing from contractors and also eliminates costly delays during construction. Believe me, the pressure of making a major color or finish decision during the remodel isn't fun for you, your contractor, or your significant other!

To help get an idea of how detailed a specification document can be, here is a sample of a kitchen & bath CRATE project data sheet that we used during the design and construction of a recent project:

Project Data Sheet

Sales Lead: Sample Salesperson | 222-333-4444
Field Lead: Sample Field Lead | 222-777-8888
Homeowner Info
    Job Name: kitchenCRATE Sample Project
    Customer: Mr. & Mrs. Sample Customer
    Job Street: Sample Adress
    Job City, State, Zip: Sample City, Sate, & Zip
    Garage Access Code: 123456
    Print Date: 01/01/21

Specifcation Format: Brand | Model | Model # | Finish

ITEM	SPECIFICATION	PURCHASED BY	INSTALLED BY
Cabinets/Hardware/Faces/Base/Trim (i.e. "wood stuff")			
Cabinet Door Faces	Flat Laminate w/ Edgebanding	Vendor	Vendor
Cabinet Drawer Faces (Island)	Flat Laminate w/ Edgebanding	Vendor	Vendor
Cabinet Frame Style	Frameless	Vendor	Vendor

ITEM	SPECIFICATION	PURCHASED BY	INSTALLED BY
Account for Undercabinet Lighting	Yes	Vendor	Vendor
Cabinet Exterior Material (Non-Island) *including underside of uppers!	Wilsonart Phantom Pearl 8211K-28	Vendor	Vendor
Cabinet Interior Material (All)	American Laminates Opti Grey	Vendor	Vendor
Cabinet Hood Material	909 Surfaces Black HD Gloss	Vendor	Vendor
Cabinet Door Hinges	All Soft Close, All Push to Open	Vendor	Vendor
Cookie Pan Divider	Yes, above appliance garage, two sets, one above and one below fixed shelf (15.5" clear height on bottom set of dividers!)	Vendor	Vendor
Shelving at Family Room	Wilsonart Phantom Pearl 8211K-28 3 - Above fireplace 1 - In fireplace niche	Vendor	Vendor
Door & Drawer Hardware	Push to Open, No Drilling!	Vendor	Vendor
Confirm Backsplash Height of 19-20"	20"	Vendor	Vendor
Toekicks	Wilsonart Phantom Pearl 8211K-28	Vendor	Vendor
Baseboard Spec and Height	1x6" flat stock to match kids bedrooms	Vendor	Vendor
Countertops			
Cantilever Distance and Direction	Island table spanning from island to cabinet end panel. Bar projecting 12" out from face of stucco to end of countertop.	Vendor	Vendor
Countertop Material Non-Island	Silestone Pietra Suede 110206 2CM	Vendor	Vendor

ITEM	SPECIFICATION	PURCHASED BY	INSTALLED BY
Honed or Polished @ Non-Island?	Honed	Vendor	Vendor
Countertop Material Island & Entertainment Center	Cambria Hadley Polished	Vendor	Vendor
Honed or Polished @ Island & Entertainment Center	Polished	Vendor	Vendor
Floating Hearth Design	14-3/8" deep, 4" tall edge, edge to match island countertop, front and one return.	Vendor	Vendor
Countertop Holes	Faucet - Center Soap - Homeowner to locate on install	Vendor	Vendor
Countertop Edge	2" mitered edge with a slight eased corner. Hearth to be a 4" mitered edge.	Vendor	Vendor
Countertop Thickness	2CM	Vendor	Vendor
Tile & Flooring			
Backsplash Field Tile	Bedrosians Allora 3" x 24" Glazed Porcelain in Solid Grey DECALLGRE324M	Vendor	Vendor
Backsplash Termination Detail	Schluter Jolly in Greige	Vendor	Vendor
Backsplash Grout Spec	Laticrete Permacolor Select	Vendor	Vendor
Backsplash Grout Color	89 Smoke Grey	Vendor	Vendor
Backsplash Grout Width	3/16"	Vendor	Vendor
Backsplash Tile Orientation	Horizontal	Vendor	Vendor

ITEM	SPECIFICATION	PURCHASED BY	INSTALLED BY
Fireplace Field Tile	Bedrosians Allora 7-3/8" x 12-3/4" Rhomboid Glazed Porcelain in Solid Grey DECALLGRERHOM	Vendor	Vendor
Fireplace Termination Detail	Schluter Jolly in Greige	Vendor	Vendor
Fireplace Accent	N/A	Vendor	Vendor
Fireplace Grout Spec	Laticrete Permacolor Select	Vendor	Vendor
Fireplace Grout Color	78 Sterling Silver	Vendor	Vendor
Fireplace Grout Width	3/16"	Vendor	Vendor
Fireplace Tile Orientation	Rhomboid	Vendor	Vendor
Floor	LVP Great California Oak RECA2204 Willow Oak 9" x 60" 8MM	Vendor	Vendor
Floor Tile Orientation & Pattern	Running length of kitchen/family room and hallway (north/south)	Vendor	Vendor
Plumbing Fixtures			
Kitchen Sink	Blanco Diamond Super Single Bowl in Concrete Gray 442752 (Drain on right)	Vendor	Vendor
Kitchen Faucet	Delta Trinsic D9159TBLDST in Matte Black	Vendor	Vendor
Kitchen Soap Dispenser	Delta Trinsic D72065TBL in Matte Black	Vendor	Vendor
Pot Fill	Delta Contemporary D1165LFBL in Matte Black	Vendor	Vendor
Kitchen Garbage Disposal	InSinkErator PRO1100XL Pro Series 1.1 HP Food Waste Garbage Disposal PRO1100XL	Vendor	Vendor

ITEM	SPECIFICATION	PURCHASED BY	INSTALLED BY
Gas Line/Appliances			
Appliances Replaced	Wall oven, cooktop, microhood	Vendor	Vendor
Old Appliance Destination	Wall oven and microhood to garage, cooktop dump, refrigerator to garage and dishwasher protected and in CRATE	Vendor	Vendor
Refrigerator (Existing)	GE PSS28KSHECSS	Vendor	Vendor
Dishwasher (Existing)	Re-use Existing	Vendor	Vendor
Wall Oven Combo (New)	KitchenAid KOCE500ESS Combo Oven	Vendor	Vendor
Warming Drawer (New) (Below Oven Combo)	KitchenAid KOWT100ESS Warming Drawer	Vendor	Vendor
Hood (New)	Zephyr Core Collection Tornado I 28" Externally Vented Range Hood - Stainless AK8100AS-BF	Vendor	Vendor
Cooktop (New)	Thermador Gas Cooktop SGSXP365TS	Vendor	Vendor
Fireplace (New)	Xtrordinair ProBuilder 54	Vendor	Vendor
Electrical			
Outlets/Switches	Gray Matte Decora No Screws Exposed at Splash, White Decora All Others	Vendor	Vendor
Lighting - Recessed	6" Wafer	Vendor	Vendor
Recessed Light Color	Soft White Glow - 3000k	Vendor	Vendor
Lighting - Pendant - Small (3)	Golden Lighting Dixon Black and Navy Seven-Inch One-Light Mini Pendant	Vendor	Vendor

ITEM	SPECIFICATION	PURCHASED BY	INSTALLED BY
Wall Sconces (4)	Golden Lighting Dixon Black and Navy Seven-Inch One-Light Wall Sconce	Vendor	Vendor
Telephone @ Kitchen	Delete and patch	Vendor	Vendor
Paint/Drywall/Stucco Texture			
Cabinet Paint #1	N/A		
Wall #1 Paint (Sheen)	Kelly Moore KM5823 City Tower	Vendor	Vendor
Ceiling Paint (Sheen)	Kelly Moore KMW57 Cloud White	Vendor	Vendor
Baseboard Paint	Kelly Moore KMW57 Cloud White	Vendor	Vendor
Mandoor Paint	Kelly Moore KMW57 Cloud White	Vendor	Vendor
Stucco	New smooth integral color stucco at entire covered back patio.	Vendor	Vendor
Framing/Steel Modifications			
Entry To Kitchen	Remove bi-fold doors, re-align opening with entry and future window, case opening for new barn door	Vendor	Vendor
Window #1 at Sink	Frame opening (60"W x 43"T) for new window, header to match header at slider, centered on sink as per drawings.	Vendor	Vendor
Window #2 at Coffee Bar	Frame opening (60"W x 43"T) for new window, header to match header at slider, centered on opening entry to kitchen.	Vendor	Vendor
Doors/Frames/Hardware/Windows			
Barn Door - Entry to Kitchen	2 @ Masonite West End Melrose Solid Core 3668	Vendor	Vendor

The "Full Set of Plans" Method

If you need to take your designing and specifying a step further, then you want to have professionally generated plans for your project.

As mentioned in "To Permit or Not to Permit," there are lots of ways to find an architect, but the AIA is the best. Check out their architect-finder tool: *aia.org/resources/6155589-find-an-architect*.

Also consider the services of a qualified interior designer, such as those who work directly with kitchen & bath CRATE on each project. Many have the tools to generate plans, schematics, and 3D renderings of your project. Others are just glorified furniture and wallpaper purchasers. Be sure to look at past documents they have generated to get a feel for the deliverable.

In general, a full set of plans includes the following:

- Demolition plan
- Floor plan
- Reflected ceiling plan (a drawing of what you would see if you lay on your floor and look up)
- Interior elevations
- Plumbing plan
- Electrical plan
- Mechanical plan

Depending on the size of the job, these plans may be combined into one sheet or even onto one drawing. For example, a small living room remodel plan might have the demolition, floor, and electrical plan all on one drawing, since there's not much to specify.

Not only will a full set of plans clarify your project in your mind and help you obtain a building permit, but it will also allow you to get accurate and comprehensive bids from contractors and subcontractors. Which just happens to be our next step.

AVOIDING THE PAIN:
No Discernable Process

A kitchen or bath remodel can take two distinct approaches.

The first is the "salad" approach of throwing the ingredients together. What's the worst that can happen? It's just a salad, after all. No big deal.

The second is the "lasagna" approach of taking it one step at a time, getting it right before you put it in the oven, and then enjoying a sensory overload—well worth the time and effort.

While there are plenty of salad remodelers out there, in our experience, people are much better off to consider their remodel as a lasagna. That's why you should follow this nine-step process to ensure you get not only a fantastic final product but also a sensible and enjoyable experience along the way.

Step 1: Phone Consultation

It starts with a simple conversation. Why? Because it's important your needs and your contractor's services align. Nothing is more frustrating for you than to host a meeting in your home only to find out what you need is not what the vendor does.

Step 2: In-home Consultation

Next, your contractor should meet with you in your home to review your project. Help them out by answering the following questions: What do you like about the space? What needs to change? How do you use the space daily and on special occasions? Only after deeply understanding your needs should your remodeler measure, photograph, and generate their jobsite notes.

Step 3: Proposal Review

Next, talk numbers. You should expect an extensive project

proposal, including a line-item project breakdown, optional items for your consideration, and extensive specifications and images for the products included in the proposal. Why discuss cost so early in the process? No one wants to design their entire project, fall in love with it, and then discover it's not in their budget.

Step 4: Cabinet Design and Countertop Selection

After reviewing the proposal and establishing the budget, it's time to design the most complicated part of the project (cabinets for kitchens) and choose the most influential design element (countertops). Your contractor should be by your side the entire way, along with a cabinet designer devoted to the smallest detail of your project. (For baths, skip this step unless it's a custom vanity.)

Step 5: Interior Design Meeting

Now that the big items are addressed, it's time to partner with an interior designer and make the vision in your head come to life. No detail is too small, and the result of this meeting should be a detailed project specification sheet that allows your contractor to manage your project with extreme accuracy during construction.

Step 6: Launch Meeting

Also known as a "Preconstruction Meeting," the launch meeting is when you receive your project schedule, review the entire job with your construction project manager, and discuss important items such as working hours, home protection, access, and pets.

Step 7: Construction

While construction can be stressful, ask your remodeler to do a few things to help alleviate this stress. First, share with them how neat and clean your project needs to be at the end of each day. Second, treat the men and women working on your project well. Doing so will send the message that you're the type of person deserving of their best work, and doing so will make the project go smoothly in the long run.

Step 8: Wrap-up

Now that your project is complete, it's time to close it out. Final payment is not required until the job is done, leaving you in financial control the entire way. Your project manager should walk the project with you at the end, making sure everything is perfect.

Step 9: Decades of Enjoyment

Once the job is complete, and you've moved back in, it's time to sit back, relax, and admire the results. Should anything come up that needs to be addressed, you must be confident your contractor will address any and all issues.

So there you go, our nine-step recipe for making the perfect remodel experience.

■ ■ ■

Chapter Recap

- Designing and specifying your project can take one of two distinct routes: creating a detailed scope document or generating a set of plans.
- If using the scope document method, evaluate your project piece by piece, and define it well.
- If generating a set of plans, consider the services of an architect or qualified interior designer.

Finding a Perfect Match for Your Project

We've specified your project with a scope document or plans, so it's time to focus on selecting your contractor.

An Important Decision

Much like choosing a spouse, business partner, or friends, choosing your contractor can be a fantastically important decision. (OK, maybe not as much as some of those, but you get the point.)

A good contractor will be your advocate, inspire trust, produce great results, and make your remodel experience anywhere from tolerable (if you hate change) to fantastic (if you have fun with these types of things).

A bad contractor will cause sleepless nights, contentious exchanges, hours sitting by the front window waiting for SOMEONE (ANYONE!) to arrive, and, at worst, lawsuits, lost money, and unfinished projects.

AVOIDING THE PAIN:
The Contractor Who Leaves You High and Dry

As I approach my tenth year running kitchen & bath CRATE, I can't help but appreciate the more than 750 past customers we've served, representing more than one thousand remodeled rooms.

And many of those customers are easy to think about because I see them regularly.

For some, "regular" is once a week. For others, it's monthly, and for still others, it's once or twice a year. But regardless, I'm thankful there's not a single one I have to avoid because we ended their project on bad terms.

That concept is key to the CRATE Way. We never want to leave a project in such a way that future interactions with that customer are awkward. That's a terrible burden, always worrying about who you might run into, or what they may be saying about you when you part ways after an abbreviated handshake and unenthusiastic pleasantries.

There are a few reasons we've kept such positive relationships with our customers, but one of the biggest is our two-year warranty. (Quite frankly, it often extends way beyond two years!) You should expect this same level of service from your contractor.

Why?

First, taking responsibility for their projects is the right thing to do. And that feels good.

Second, they should want to be your contractor for life. If they're playing the long game, it means they're building a business for fifty years, not five.

Third, it sets them apart. I can't tell you how often I hear stories about the "other guys" you can't track down should a problem arise a year, a month, or even a day after they receive final payment. Yes, they're in a business where doing the right thing is all it takes to be different. (Sad, right?)

So before you sign a contract or commence construction, make sure you have a detailed warranty policy from your contractor. It will give you peace of mind and help you avoid future issues.

There are two distinct ways to choose a contractor, and it's a huge mistake to confuse the two. You can't have it both ways. Either you negotiate with one contractor you feel comfortable with, or you "hard bid" your project to multiple contractors and make your decision mostly based on price. Either way can work well, but you can't do both. Let's tackle the more common method first.

Choosing Your Contractor Via Bidding

Bidding your project is the most common way of choosing a contractor, especially for large-scale, multimonth projects. As with any value proposition, you must be careful, because you get what you pay for. Back when the kitchen & bath CRATE team used to do large-scale custom remodeling work (we now focus exclusively on kitchen & bath CRATE), one of our project categories was the "Post-Low-Bid-Contractor Repair Job." These were jobs for clients who started out with the low bidder (sometimes REALLY low), commenced work, and then had their contractor (1) never show up, (2) take a deposit and run, or (3) "complete" the job in a frighteningly bad fashion.

But there *is* a right way to bid your job out, and here it is:

1. Ensure your scope of work documents are in place. See "Designing and Specifying" for the details, using either a

scope document for simple, smaller jobs or plans for larger, more detailed jobs.

2. Find three good contractors willing to bid. Bear in mind, most of the best residential contractors will respectfully decline bid invitations, depending on workflow. They know they'll never be the low bidder because of supply and demand: their services are in demand and therefore their prices are higher. However, plenty of residential contractors are eager to bid. Use web searches, HomeAdvisor, Houzz, social media sites, or word of mouth to come up with a list, and then . . .

3. Check references! Yes, that's right: ask for three references. And not just three references, but the names and phone numbers for *the last three clients* they worked with, including project dates. Why? Otherwise you'll get their three favorite clients, not objective clients who recently experienced this contractor's services. Many contractors have performed well in the past, but you're interested in current performance. Also, by getting project dates, you validate the recency of the job and find out if the contractor has been slow for a while (if they have been, investigate why).

4. Now you're armed with your list of three qualified contractors, and it's time to host a job walk. We recommend having the contractors walk the job at the same time. This allows everyone to hear answers to questions posed by others and creates a sense of competition among the bidders. Make sure you have copies of your scope documents for the contractors.

5. After walking the job, set a firm bid date for the project. We recommend two weeks as the ideal time frame for most jobs. This allows the contractors time to assemble the budget and solicit pricing from subcontractors and suppliers. A firm date creates their first deadline. Buyer beware: if your

contractor is late getting you a bid, don't expect them to be timely in starting (or finishing) your project.

6. Once the bids are in, it's time to evaluate the proposals. Be sure to request the bids be broken out by trade or sections of the project (framing, plumbing, electrical, drywall). This helps you analyze each contractor's assumptions. If a line item doesn't look right, ask for clarification. In our experience, if something doesn't look right, it probably isn't.

7. Now that the bids are evaluated, it's time to make your decision. By this time, you've met each contractor, interacted with them, reviewed their pricing, and clarified their bid. You should have a good feeling about your direction. If not, if there is no clear winner, congratulations! Looks like you have more than one good option. So go ahead and make your choice.

8. What's the first thing you ask for from your newly hired contractor? A schedule, of course. Ask for a complete project schedule (See sample next page) showing a firm start date and timing for each item of the project. Once again, this is a chance for your contractor to meet a deadline. If they won't send you a schedule, or they send one later than requested, consider it an ominous sign. (See example schedule on the next page.)

9. Last, and MOST IMPORTANT, it's time to sign a contract. We highly recommend paying the $30 and using an AIA contract. These contracts are the best in the business, and they protect the homeowner to no end. You can buy single contracts at the AIA website: *https://www.aiacontracts.org/*. For a residential job, the A105 is perfect. We've used it for years. If your contractor insists on using their contract, be sure to review carefully. It's likely written with their interests in mind.

Sample Schedule	start	end	
	02/04/21	03/05/21	
Move Contents	02/04	02/04	Move Contents :: Homeowner
Set kitchenCRATE	02/04	02/04	Set kitchenCRATE :: Vendor
Set Temp Toilet	02/04	02/04	Set Temp Toilet :: Vendor
Floor Protection	02/05	02/05	Floor Protection :: kitchenCRATE
Set Dust Control	02/05	02/05	Set Dust Control :: kitchenCRATE
Demolition	02/05	02/08	Demolition :: kitchenCRATE
Lighting Rough-in	02/08	02/08	Lighting Rough-in :: kitchenCRATE
Plumbing/Electrical Rough-in	02/09	02/11	Plumbing/Electrical Rough-in :: kitchenCRATE
Hang Sheetrock	02/09	02/11	Hang Sheetrock :: kitchenCRATE
Sheetrock Mud, Tape & Texture	02/11	02/15	Sheetrock Mud, Tape & Texture :: kC Refinish
Custom Cabinet Installation	02/15	02/17	Custom Cabinet Installation :: Vendor
Plywood Subtop Install	02/16	02/16	Plywood Subtop Install :: Vendor
Countertop Template	02/17	02/17	Countertop Template :: Vendor
Countertop Layout Meeting	02/18	02/18	Countertop Layout Meeting :: Vendor
Paint Cabinets	02/18	02/22	Paint Cabinets :: kC Refinish
Paint Doors/Drawers	02/18	02/24	Paint Doors/Drawers :: kC Refinish
Countertop Fabrication	02/19	02/24	Countertop Fabrication :: Vendor
Wall/Ceiling Paint	02/22	02/24	Wall/Ceiling Paint :: kC Refinish
Sink & Countertop Install	02/25	02/25	Sink & Countertop Install :: Vendor
Backsplash Install	02/26	03/01	Backsplash Install :: Vendor
Baseboard Install	03/02	03/02	Baseboard Install :: kitchenCRATE
Finish Electrical	03/02	03/03	Finish Electrical :: kitchenCRATE
Finish Plumbing	03/02	03/03	Finish Plumbing :: kitchenCRATE
Appliance Install	03/03	03/03	Appliance Install :: kitchenCRATE
Re-install Doors/Drawers	03/04	03/04	Re-install Doors/Drawers :: kitchenCRATE
Final Clean	03/05	03/05	Final Clean :: kitchenCRATE
Final Inspection	03/05	03/05	Final Inspection :: City

Sample Project Schedule in Gantt Format

Choosing Your Contractor Via Negotiation

This method of choosing your contractor follows a similar course as the one above, but it offers a few key advantages and some disadvantages.

The key advantage is forging a trusting relationship with your contractor early. If you choose the right builder, this will be an enjoyable, productive experience—and much quicker than the bid process. A good contractor who knows he or she is the "chosen one" will treat your job with urgency and respect, knowing that you are placing much trust in them.

Negotiating a project still requires a scope document, reference checks (even more so!), a job walk, and a bidding phase, but the spirit will be one of collaboration and win-win, as opposed to adversarial and competitive. Once again, to each their own.

At kitchen & bath CRATE, we don't hard bid projects. We prefer to build relationships. The main concern we hear from homeowners is, "How do I know I'm getting a good deal?" It's a great question.

We solve this through an open-book estimating process. The way we see it, this method gets the homeowner a great deal and establishes a good working relationship from the onset. Pretty nice indeed.

AVOIDING THE PAIN:
"Fuzzy Math" and Lump-Sum Pricing

Imagine you're at the grocery store. You pick out your items and mosey to the checkout line. The clerk rings you up. However, the cash register does not tally your total as your groceries pass through the scanner. Instead, the screen is blank. Upon scanning the final item, the clerk tells you the bill is $300 even.

Hmm, that's odd, you think to yourself.

So you ask the clerk for a receipt, and they print one out. It says: "Groceries. All of them. $300."

It would be hard to trust the final price, would it not?

Sometimes I can't help but chuckle when customers describe "proposals" they get from the "other guys." While they aren't necessarily written on the proverbial back of a napkin, they indeed leave a lot to be desired.

My favorites are the ones that are some form of "kitchen remodel, including demo, drywall, cabinets, countertops" followed by the cost . . .

That's it. That's the entire description. It's just so fascinating to me!

So be sure to ask your contractor for a complete, down-to-the-dollar proposal, including a detailed scope of work description. Let's face it: if you're going to spend a significant amount of money on a remodel project, you'll want to know where every dollar and cent is going. It's your money after all, right?

■　■　■

Chapter Recap

- Choosing your contractor can be a fantastically important decision.
- Option One: Choose your contractor via bidding.
- Option Two: Choose your contractor via negotiation.

Timing Your Remodel to Fit Your Life

You're really on your way now! Your contractor is on board, so now it's time to schedule your project.

When you start your remodel depends on two timing factors: timing based on your life circumstances and timing based on seasons (weather). Here we go!

Accommodating Life Circumstances

The first timing factor is easy to understand. After all, who would start remodeling their home when they have an important upcoming event or are about to host a major holiday?

Um, well, a lot of people, actually.

That's right: in our experience mild amnesia occurs as homeowners are about to embark on a remodel. Sometimes they are so engrossed in the process that they forget that their first grandchild is due in five weeks, or they fail to recall that they're hosting a graduation party for 150 of their closest friends and family in about a month.

So do this: take the project schedule your contractor provided in "Choosing a Contractor" and add 20 percent to it. (Example: If the schedule is forty calendar days, use forty-eight calendar days for this exercise.) Then sit down with your household and review each day of your personal schedules, from the day your project starts until the end of this 120 percent timeline.

That's right. Each day. You'd be amazed at the things you remember when you go through this together.

AVOIDING THE PAIN:
Remodels That Take Too Long

Based on the 750 or so potential customers I screen each year, I'd guess "fear of the long remodel project" to be the biggest factor in people delaying a renovation.

Perhaps you feel the same. You're just unsure if you can get through a remodel project that goes longer than expected.

A few factors are at the heart of this very reasonable apprehension. Here are the main time-related concerns we hear from potential customers:

- Remodels are disruptive to family life, and long remodels get exponentially more disruptive by the day.
- A remodel with an unknown duration makes planning life events (hosting, vacations, holidays, kid events) very frustrating.

- There's a feeling of helplessness if a job goes too long and they don't have any recourse.
- There's the embarrassment of mentioning to friends and family that the remodel still isn't finished . . .

We're well aware of these pain points for customers. Here's how your contractor can help ease your minds and make sure you don't deal with a delayed project:

- Have your project manager provide a detailed, day-by-day project schedule to you weeks before the project begins. This allows you to track your project during construction.
- Ask for a $250-per-day project-completion guarantee. This means that for any working day your project goes long, you get $250 off the final invoice. This should be industry standard. I mean, why would a contractor not stand behind their finish date?
- Ensure they order all project materials well before the job starts, and avoid starting a renovation until all materials are on hand. This avoids the all-too-typical delay because "we're waiting on your [insert material] to arrive . . ."

As you can see, the timing of your project should be taken VERY seriously. Why? Because what's important to you should be important to them.

Accommodating the Weather

As with the previous factor, this too should be obvious for folks to assess. Alas, once again, we often encounter full exterior projects starting in late fall.

Here's a good rule of thumb: don't open up your roof, exterior walls, or windows if there is a chance of rain in the near future. (As an aside, there are certain climates that are "never" dry, so make sure you have a contractor experienced with wet-weather work.)

To further assist, here is a list of items to avoid in wet weather:

- Exterior concrete
- Pool plastering
- Major dirt movement or landscaping
- Roof or wall framing
- Roofing
- Gutter replacement
- Window replacement
- Stucco work
- Exterior painting

In addition, be sure your contractor protects the inside of your home if doing work during wet months. The constant tracking of water and mud through the house can cause a mess and even permanent damage.

A pro tip regarding floor protection: be leery of the material used when covering floors. Red rosin paper has been known, when wet, to bleed onto carpet or linoleum. Also, adhesive-backed carpet covering (a thin plastic that sticks to carpet) can leave an adhesive residue that attracts dirt over time and can leave a stain. Ram Board and Masonite are the two best forms of flooring protection to use on hard surfaces. The bottom line is that it takes an experienced pro to match the proper flooring protection with the flooring type.

■ ■ ■

Chapter Recap

- *When* you start your remodel depends on two timing factors: timing based on your life circumstances and timing based on seasons (weather).
- Consider all upcoming life events.
- Consider how the season, and specifically weather, might affect your project.

Advice for Enduring a Home Renovation

Here's some advice for getting through the remodel process while maintaining your sanity.

Expect the Inevitable Problem

The one thing you can be sure of during your remodel: there will be a problem.

Not necessarily a big problem, and certainly not an unsolvable problem, but there will be a problem. Material may arrive damaged. One of your selections might appear different from the sample you chose. Mold could be discovered once the walls are opened up. Any variety of challenges may be encountered.

Your best game plan is to expect problems during the job. That's the nature of construction. (And why the life expectancy of most contractors is roughly forty-two years . . .)

Trust the Professionals

When problems pop up, be confident in your team. If you've followed the previous chapters, you'll have a great contractor and design team, so let them help you through the process.

In fact, the main difference between an average contractor and a great contractor is the ability to navigate challenges.

Another element of trusting the pros is to show that you trust by not micromanaging. This is a fine line. The remodel, after all, is yours. And you're paying good money and expecting a high-quality product. So expecting excellence is not the issue. But micromanaging and expecting excellence are two different things.

The topic of micromanaging reminds me of one past customer. Let's call him "Daryl."

Daryl was recently retired. Daryl was a marine veteran. Daryl had a lot of time on his hands.

Daryl, bless his heart, would literally pull up a chair at the entrance to his kitchen and watch the entire project happen. Every minute of every day. The man's bladder must have been the size of Montana. I admit, our team was quite intimidated. There he sat, day in and day out, tattooed arms crossed, scowling like an ominous statue, ready to pounce at signs of the smallest mistake.

Near the end of the job his project manager, who had broken through Daryl's icy personality a bit, asked him why he'd sat there for nearly three weeks but never said anything. "Why would I say anything?" Daryl asked. "I was the one learning how to remodel from the guys that knew what they were doing!"

The entire job we thought he was checking up on us, when really he was just bored and wanting to watch a real-life HGTV show in his own home.

AVOIDING THE PAIN:
Untrustworthy Strangers in Your Home

You probably don't LOVE the idea of strangers in your home. They are, after all, strange to you. Part of the definition, right?

So you probably REALLY don't love ill-mannered, rude, or vulgar strangers in your home, right?

I'm continually amazed by our customers' stories regarding past experiences with contractors in their homes. From inappropriate language to theft and everything in between.

And that's why you should expect your contractor to self-perform as much of their work as possible. The following are common items that should be self-performed by a contractor's crews:

- Demolition
- Rough carpentry
- Finish carpentry
- Vanity installation
- Door installation
- Sheetrock hanging
- Drywall tape and texturing
- Cabinet refinishing
- Painting
- Cabinet hardware installation
- Plumbing rough and finish
- Electrical rough and finish
- Final clean

Furthermore, your contractor must run background checks on employees before extending an employment offer. It may add additional time and expense to their recruiting efforts, but it's the right thing to do for their customers.

And for any items your contractor outsources, they should

use only the best installers and fabricators. And give them bonus points for having used the same subcontractors for over a decade. That's a sure sign they have a strong working relationship.

The bottom line: during your remodel you will have strangers in your home. It's up to your contractor to be sure they are safe and reliable strangers. After all, your safety, and that of your family, is paramount. You should expect nothing less.

But Be Sure to Check on Them

It's highly recommended, however, that you check your project daily. This is easy if you're living in the home during construction. However, if you're remodeling a second home, or have moved out during the remodel, be sure you check in daily to make sure things look as you expect. Catching an issue early helps make the repair or change simple and affordable for all parties.

A good idea regarding this issue is creating a project notepad. Purchase an inexpensive notepad or notebook before the job starts, and each night put your requests/reminders/concerns down on the pad. Instruct your contractor to check the notepad each morning before starting work and to call you if there are further questions. Not only does this create a seamless line of communication, but it also establishes a written record of items if you ever need to go back and validate.

AVOIDING THE PAIN:
Disrespect for Your Property

I can recall an evening many years ago when we hosted another family at our home. We love this family, and to this day, we're close friends with them. But this family consisted of two parents and three boys. And these boys were, well, boys. They were energetic, loud, and all in all quite a handful. (They've matured into fine young men, by the way!)

Toward the end of the evening, we heard the dreaded sound of silence. Any parent knows that when an unruly group of boys goes quiet, it's not right.

Our investigation into the silence revealed quite a scene: one of the boys had climbed to the top of the closet insert as though it were a ladder, another had removed 100 percent of the contents from 100 percent of the furniture pieces, and the third was so very proud of himself because he had fed the fish. Hand lotion. (The fish did not survive the meal.)

So when it comes to treating a home with care and concern, I can't help but remember that night and how I, as the home-owner, felt a bit violated by these little angels.

Our homes are quite an intimate place, are they not?

It's where we raise our family, host our guests, break bread, laugh, cry, celebrate, and mourn. Yes, it's probably the most important space in our daily life.

So it's understandable to be a bit nervous about opening our homes to strangers. And we get this. This is why you should expect your contractor to take what we call "remarkable responsibility."

Quite simply, remarkable responsibility means treating your home as if it were their own. Here are a few specific ways they can do so:

- At your preconstruction meeting (we call it a "launch meeting"), your project manager should cover an assortment of topics with you, from pets to working hours to parking, to be sure they're operating in the most convenient way possible for your day-to-day life.
- Expect them to arrive on time, every day, and make sure

they communicate their arrival time with you in a manner of your choosing.

- Before they commence demolition, make sure they fully enclose your project work area with plastic and use fans to create negative air pressure, significantly reducing the amount of dust entering the rest of your home.
- Encourage them to use an assortment of materials and methods to protect your flooring from foot traffic or items that may accidentally drop.
- When moving appliances, be sure they wrap them carefully and use specialty moving equipment such as air sleds and lifting straps.
- As you would be told when visiting a national park, tell them to abide by a "leave no trace" mantra, so no one will be washing out tile grout buckets in your planters!

There are many more ways in which your contractor can treat your home as if it were their own. After all, you deserve *remarkable*, and that's what they should deliver.

Remember, Nearly Everything Is Fixable

If you encounter an issue, be sure to pause, take a deep breath, and remember that nearly everything is fixable.

If a work of art that's been in your family for two years gets damaged, of course that's not fixable. (And of course you would never leave such an item in a spot where it could get damaged.) But nearly everything else can be fixed or altered if it's not as it should be. Remember this as you navigate problems, and it will do wonders for your stress level.

A pro tip regarding preparing your home for demolition: make sure you remove any breakables and/or wall hangings on the opposite side of the wall from any demolition area. Demolition causes vibration, and vibration causes things to move and/or become dislodged. So be sure to clear both the demolition area *and* the walls of the adjacent rooms!

Make It Fun and Show Appreciation

Keep in mind that you're getting a painless remodel! (After all, that's what this book is called.)

Focus on the finish line and have fun. Buy the crew lunch every once in a while to show your appreciation. I guarantee you'll get a better product and have happier workers, and it will cost only a few bucks.

Our crews love to come back to the office at the end of their shifts and tell us stories about our generous customers. Our crews have received fresh-baked cookies, an ungodly number of doughnuts, DoorDash lunches, DoorDash breakfasts, a brisket that had been smoking for over ten hours, wine, beer, gift cards, and an assortment of other forms of gratitude. It means so much to them and makes their ten-hour days so well worth it.

AVOIDING THE PAIN:
Your Home Treated as a Jobsite

You and I can probably agree that, during a home-renovation project, the "temperature" rises a bit. And by temperature I mean stress level. No matter how carefully your contractor coordinates your project, no matter how much care and concern they take with each task, no matter what is said or done or promised, it's still more stressful than the average day, right?

One thing that exacerbates the stress is clutter. And not your clutter, but your contractor's clutter.

So when we launched the kitchen & bath CRATE concept way back in 2012, we decided we'd differentiate ourselves in this regard. Here are a few things we do to minimize our clutter during construction. We suggest asking your remodeler to implement these same items:

- The CRATE helps us keep all our tools and most of your materials out of your house. (The CRATE is the large, 8' x 16' container we set in front of each project, filled with the equipment and materials needed to do the job.) Each night we pack it all away, and each morning we bring it back out. Doing so allows our customers to maximize their enjoyable space during the times we're not working.
- We have a "sock rule." It goes like this: we need to leave the project clean enough each night that our customers can walk into the work area with socks on and not detect any debris. That's why we vacuum our work area at the end of each day, ensure things are arranged in a neat and orderly manner, and do our best to impress you, even before we're done.
- While it's impossible to eliminate dust during construction completely, our clients deserve our best efforts to keep it at a minimum. That's why our team is quick and efficient in setting up plastic dust walls and ensuring we have air movement into our job site and out a door or window. These tactics alone dramatically reduce dust impact on the home.

It's our job to do all we can to reduce the temperature during construction. We hope you agree!

■ ■ ■

Chapter Recap

- The one thing you can be sure of during your remodel: there will be a problem.
- Be confident in your team and don't micromanage.
- But check your project daily.
- Show appreciation.

How to Protect Yourself During Your Project

Time to get your paperwork in order. Let's look at the most important documents you can have in place during your project.

Contract Documents

What they are: Contract documents are a general term describing the documents on which your contract is based. In many cases, the contract documents are a set of plans. In some cases, the contract documents are simply a scope of work. Either way, contract documents are the documents your contract references. They define your project.

Why they're important: Without contract documents, the scope of work exists only in the mind of the client and the contractor. Not only are the two minds often of differing opinions, but if there is ever a need for a legal remedy, no contract documents means no leg to stand on.

How you get them: See "Designing and Specifying," where we discussed the development of your contract documents, including two different ways to define your project.

When they should be in place: Before the project starts.

Prime Contract

What it is: A prime contract is a legal agreement between a project owner and a general contractor. At minimum, it defines the project price, schedule, payment terms, and ramifications if either party fails to uphold their end of the agreement. It also references the contract documents described above as an integral part of the contract.

Why it's important: It protects you, plain and simple. Without a contract, it's nearly impossible to seek legal remedy to an issue.

How you get it: Any general contractor worth their salt will have a standard agreement. Be sure you review it in great detail, as it needs to protect you as well as the general contractor. Alternatively, the AIA has a great set of legal documents that can be purchased for less than $40 each. We recommend the AIA's A105 for almost all residential projects if the general contractor does not have a standard contract you agree with.

When it should be in place: Before the project starts.

Project Schedule

What it is: A document that shows each element of your project, along with a start and end date for each. Professional schedules are usually in a Gantt chart format but can also be a simple bullet-point document. See sample schedule on page 50.

Why it's important: Without a detailed schedule it's nearly impossible to hold your contractor accountable until it's too late. It's much better to notice schedule slippage on an item-by-item basis than it is at the end of a job.

How you get it: Ask your contractor to generate it. If they cannot produce it, or do not understand what you mean, start looking elsewhere. It's like a mechanic who struggles to find your hood-release button. ("Um, I think I'll take my car somewhere else . . .")

When it should be in place: Before the project starts.

Insurance Certificate

What it is*:* A certificate produced by a contractor's insurance carrier proving insurance coverage.

Why it's important: Without this document it's difficult to prove your contractor carries insurance. Also, when listed as "additionally insured" at the bottom-left of the certificate, an owner benefits from additional risk reduction if an on-the-job accident occurs.

How you get it: Ask your general contractor to provide this document from their insurance agent. Not being able to provide this document is a major warning sign. (Enough to where you should probably not use this contractor.)

When it should be in place: Before the project starts.

Contractor's License

What it is: A state-issued license proving a contractor has the education, experience, and (sometimes) insurance necessary to perform contracting activities.

Why it's important: An unlicensed contractor exposes the project owner to an array of liabilities. For example, an unlicensed contractor has not been qualified by the state licensing board, and therefore the licensing board can offer little help during a dispute. A contractor that has not taken the time to acquire a license obviously does not place importance on following rules and regulations. This is a concern on any project, because compliance ensures safety for occupants.

How you get it: Ask your contractor for a copy of their "pocket license," a credit card–size license that shows class and expiration date. In addition, check your state licensing board website to cross-reference any information provided by your contractor.

When it should be in place: Before the project starts.

Preliminary Notice (or "Prelien")

What it is: A document filed by *subcontractors* that notifies you, the property owner, that they are working on your job and reserve the right to lien your property if they are not paid by your general contractor.

CALIFORNIA PRELIMINARY NOTICE
In accordance with section 8102, 8202 and 9303, California Civil Code. THIS IS NOT A LIEN.
This is NOT a reflection on the integrity of any contractor or subcontractor.

**CONSTRUCTION LENDER OR
REPUTED CONSTRUCTION LENDER**

Name and address of claimant giving notice:

has furnished or will furnish labor, service, equipment or material of the following general description:

**OWNER OR
REPUTED OWNER(S)/PUBLIC ENTITY**

Description of job site sufficient for identification:

The name of the person or firm who contracted for the purchase of such labor, service, equipment or material furnished is:

An estimate of the total price of the labor, service, equipment or material provided or to be provided is:
$

**DIRECT CONTRACTOR OR
REPUTED DIRECT CONTRACTOR**

NOTICE TO PROPERTY OWNER
EVEN THOUGH YOU HAVE PAID YOUR CONTRACTOR IN FULL, if the person or firm that has given you this notice is not paid in full for labor, service, equipment, or material provided or to be provided to your construction project, a lien may be placed on your property. Foreclosure of the lien may lead to loss of all or part of your property. You may wish to protect yourself against this by (1) requiring your contractor to provide a signed release by the person or firm that has given you this notice before making payment to your contractor, or (2) any other method that is appropriate under the circumstances.
    This notice is required by law to be served by the undersigned as a statement of your legal rights. This notice is not intended to reflect upon the financial condition of the contractor or the person employed by you on the construction project.
    If you record a notice of cessation or completion of your construction project, you must within 10 days after recording, send a copy of the notice of completion to your contractor and the person or firm that has given you this notice. The notice must be sent by registered or certified mail. Failure to send the notice will extend the deadline to record a claim of lien. You are not required to send the notice if you are a residential homeowner of a dwelling containing four or fewer units.

OTHER

Date:

Signature:

Why it's important: Since the subcontractors do not have a direct contract with you, the property owner, the law states they have to tell you they have future lien rights if they are not paid by your general contractor. Not every subcontractor files a prelien, but many do, just in case. **THIS IS NOT A LIEN!** It is simply a notice of the potential for a lien if your contractor does not pay.

How you get it: The subcontractor has to mail it to you within a certain number of days of starting work. The number of days varies by jurisdiction, but it is usually around twenty. When you get these, simply file them away for use at the end of the job. See the next section on lien release.

When it should be in place: You should have all of the preliens by the end of the job, for subcontractors securing their prelien rights. If you don't get one from a subcontractor, no action is required.

Lien Release

What it is: A lien release is an official document that releases you, the property owner, from lien responsibility. There are many different kinds of lien releases, but the most important is an unconditional upon final lien release.

UNCONDITIONAL WAIVER AND RELEASE UPON FINAL PAYMENT

Civil Code Section 3262(d)(4)

The undersigned has been paid in full for all labor, services, equipment or material furnished to <u>Mr. & Mrs. Sample Customer</u> located at <u>Sample Address, Sample City, Sample State, Sample Zip</u> and does hereby release any mechanic's lien, stop notice or any right against a labor and material bond on the job, except for disputed claims for extra work in the amount of $<u>XX,XXX.XX</u>.

Date: <u>XX-XX-XX</u>

D. Scott Monday
CEO
Kitchen & bath CRATE

Why it's important: Once your general contractor and subcontractors provide you this document, they waive their right to a lien.

How you get it: Collect an unconditional upon final lien release from each subcontractor and supplier that has filed a prelien on your property, and then from your general contractor. Parties only provide this document concurrent with receiving final payment, since it removes their lien rights. The reason this is so important to secure from subcontractors who have preliened is because it ensures your general contractor has paid them in full (and ensures they won't come after you for payment if the general contractor flees with your money).

When it should be in place: You should get these from your general contractor concurrent with handing them final payment.

Notice of Completion

What it is: An official document filed with your county clerk's office stating your project is complete.

Why it's important: It starts the clock on your contractor's lien rights expiring. Check your local law, but anywhere from thirty to ninety days after it is filed, your property can't be liened by a contractor (unless they have done so already). This protects you from any liens being filed long after your project is complete.

How you get it: Check your local legal document store for the right form used in your jurisdiction.

When it should be in place: It should be filed within a few days of your project ending.

Now you're aware of all the documents you need to effectively administer your remodel. It may seem like a lot of paperwork, but most is provided by your contractor before the job begins. It's well worth spending some time on these items to ensure you have the proper protection in place.

■ ■ ■

Chapter Recap

Keep track of the following documents:
- Contract documents
- Prime contract
- Project schedule
- Insurance certificate
- Contractor's license
- Prelien
- Lien release
- Notice of completion

Tips for Closing Out Your Project

Sometimes crossing the finish line on your project is the hardest part. The last few details can be so frustrating! You want your project complete (and so does your contractor), but little items keep popping up, and pretty soon you feel like the job will never end. There are a few things you and your contractor can do to get to the finish line. Some are based on concepts we've covered, and others are new.

Respect the Finish Date

In "Important Documents," we talked about the project schedule—a sacred, contractor-issued document that shows when each element of your project should be completed.

When you get this schedule, look at the finish date. Then put this date in your calendar. Then remind your contractor of this date weekly until the project is done. **Don't let this date die.** This date is important, because if it's forgotten, before you know it, your project is behind schedule, and the date is a distant memory.

There's really no purpose in creating a schedule and then not holding the team accountable for meeting it, so make sure you constantly check.

Create a Punch List

A punch list is a list of the items that need to be completed before the project owner deems the project complete.

Any good contractor endeavors to have a "zero punch list" project; meaning items are completed as they are noticed, not left to linger until the job is complete. (Beware if your contractor says over and over, "We'll take care of that at the end." This is just like your kid telling you they'll clean their room later . . .)

Alas, most projects have a few items that are not noticed until the job is substantially complete and cleaned up. No matter how many times you look at a job during construction, there are usually items you just didn't notice.

It's imperative to have a "punch walk" with your contractor right at the end of the job. Ideally, you'll have this walk after the work is complete, after the job is cleaned, and before you provide final payment. It's a good idea for both the project owner and contractor to make a list, or create one and then run a copy to ensure both parties agree.

It may also be helpful to take pictures of each item as you list them, just so there's additional backup in case you need to refer back.

Your contractor should begin completing the punch list items immediately after the list is created.

\multicolumn{5}{c}{**Punch List**}

Who	Priority	Room	Item	Done?
Vendor	1	Family	Adjust all outlets and switches so they are proper depth and so plates are flush against wall/tile, etc.	☐
Vendor	1	Family	Adjust all drawers for proper open.	☐
Vendor	1	Kitchen	Adjust all drawers for proper open.	☐
Vendor	1	Family	Patch wall right of fireplace just above hearth.	☐
Vendor	1	Family	Caulk connection front face, left side of two lower floating shelves.	☐
Vendor	1	Roof	Spray paint exhaust cover inside chimney cap so stainless steel is not visible.	☐
Vendor	2	Family	Install IR receiver.	☐
Vendor	2	Kitchen	Fix and reinstall coffee bar drawers.	☐
Vendor	2	Kitchen	Middle drawer left of cooktop keeps popping out	☐
Vendor	3	Kitchen	Please raise nested portion of drawer so it's flush with top edge of lower box; adjust slides so bottom right consistently sits flush	☐
Vendor	3	Kitchen	Nested drawer under cooktop not closing flush on right side	☐
Vendor	3	Kitchen	Center drawer, center bank scraping and causing damage.	☐
Vendor	4	Kitchen	Sand, prime and paint walls. Paint in garage; polished limestone.	☐
Vendor	4	Kitchen	Supply and install adjustable shelves at island.	☐
Vendor	4	Entry	Paint inside edges of doors	☐
Vendor	4	Family	Patch ceiling ding near slider.	☐
Vendor	4	Laundry	Touch up wall right edge of exit door, hidden by washer	☐
Vendor	5	Patio	Touch-up paint, including painting new eave vent frames.	☐
Vendor	5	Hall	Replace return air filters.	☐
Vendor	6	Family	Seal tile at fireplace.	☐
Vendor	6	Family	Clean grout off of fireplace frame.	☐

Vendor	6	Family	Clean all LED light lenses.	☐
Vendor	7	Family	Vacuum out floor vent.	☐
Vendor	7	Kitchen	Remove grout at bottom of splash. Painter to caulk 4/8.	☐
Vendor	7	Kitchen	Clean all LED light lenses.	☐
Vendor	8	Kitchen	Blind corner cabinet door needs to be adjusted to be flush along bottom edge	☐
Vendor	9	Kitchen	Tech Drawer: Face not plumb, push-to-open not working, drawer not closing.	☐
Vendor	9	Kitchen	Drawer below ovens not closing fully.	☐
Vendor	9	Bath	Sand, prime and paint ceiling.	☐
Vendor	9	Bath	Sand, prime and paint walls. Paint in garage, polished limestone.	☐
Vendor	9	Family	Touch-up paint around fan.	☐
Vendor	9	Family	Caulk hearth to wall on right side.	☐
Vendor	9	Patio	Paint at top of old dining room slider.	☐
Vendor	9	Patio	Paint foundation vents	☐
Vendor	9	Patio	Paint outside of new door from bathroom to patio.	☐
Vendor	9	Entry	Paint window stop.	☐
Vendor	9	Family	Fix grout discoloration at fireplace.	☐

Conduct a Punch List Follow-up Walk

Once your contractor indicates the punch list is complete, you should walk the job with him or her. Pull out your list and go through each item, ensuring it's complete to your satisfaction.

If the list is complete, then your contractor should be paid promptly.

Nothing is as frustrating to a contractor as completing a punch list and then having payment withheld for "one more item I just noticed."

Will items that need to be fixed pop up after you make final payment?

Sure, on occasion, but under no circumstance should final payment be withheld from a contractor because you keep finding one more small thing. If you're concerned your contractor will not service your project postpayment, then you picked the wrong contractor. If you're still concerned, then hold back a small amount of the final payment until the last item is complete.

And this leads nicely into our last point . . .

Be Careful Before Releasing Final Payment

If you've followed our advice throughout this book, the end of the job should be as pleasant as the beginning and middle.

But there are a lot of deadbeat contractors out there, so if you've made the wrong choice or were fooled in the beginning, you may need to play hardball.

Don't release final payment until you're satisfied with your project.

But be careful and ensure your level of satisfaction would hold up to an arbitrator, judge, or jury, because that's the road you may be on. If you're withholding $10,000 from your contractor because a door has a scratch, you're not playing fair. Figure out the cost to make the repair (if your contractor is responsible for the damage), then double it and withhold that amount. That way you have the money to make the fix, but you're not unreasonably holding funds.

A warning about dangerous payment practices: I can't tell you how many folks I've spoken with over the years who have shared some variation of "my contractor took all my money and never finished the job." Many states (including California) actually make it illegal for contractors to collect large deposits or collect more money than the work they've performed. So know your rights. A great rule of thumb is to never pay out more than the work you've received. For example, if your job is 50 percent complete, don't pay out more than 50 percent of the contract amount.

If your contractor cites "cash flow" issues, it means one of three things: (1) They are using current projects to cash flow future projects, (2) They have poor vendor relationships and therefore are not on adequate terms with their suppliers, and/or (3) They are financially insolvent. Believe me, all these are huge red flags and should cause you much concern regarding your contractor's ability to perform.

■ ■ ■

Chapter Recap

- Hold the team accountable for the schedule.
- Create a punch list and have a "punch walk."
- Conduct a punch list follow-up walk.
- Don't release final payment until you're satisfied with your project.

After the Project Is Complete

You're done! Now let's look at some postproject items you may encounter.

Warranty Items/Issues

A key reason for choosing a reputable contractor is often most evident after the project is complete. Good contractors address warranty items promptly and thoroughly. Bad contractors are nowhere to be found when an issue comes up.

In terms of the letter of the law, contractors are required to warranty the workmanship of the project for a specific period of time. In California, this is one year. If a workmanship issue pops up within one year, your contractor has to make the repair. If not, they risk a claim being filed with the licensing board in addition to legal action.

Since you chose a great contractor, you'll likely get fantastic service and support well beyond one year. After all, the contractor's reputation is at stake, and good business practices (not to mention common human decency) dictate customer service is paramount for future referrals.

One note: This warranty will not cover defective materials. The manufacturer's warranty on materials in your project transfers to you once the project is complete. Your contractor should be willing and able to assist you through the repair process, but remember that you own the warranty and have ultimate authority with the manufacturer.

Wrap-up Meeting

When the dust settles from your project, when the punch list is complete, when final payment is made, when you've had a little while to live in and enjoy your project, it's a good idea to have a wrap-up meeting. During this meeting each party can check in, and any after-the-punch-list items can be addressed. Most important, you can offer feedback to your contractor.

Perhaps you noticed something during construction that they could improve. Perhaps the contractor did something remarkable that you noted. Perhaps you have general feedback regarding the process. No matter what, this short conversation can leave both parties knowing that everything is on the table, and it is extraordinarily valuable to your contractor. Consider it a small gift for a job well done.

Contractor Reviews

Finally, the most important thing you can do for your contractor is to provide a review. Ideally, this would be a short, two-to-three-paragraph review answering some or all of these questions:

- What was the best part of working with your contractor?

- If you referred your contractor to a friend, how would you describe them?
- Did your contractor surprise or delight you in some way?

The most helpful way to provide this review is to email it to your contractor (for publication on marketing materials) and post it to an online review site (Google, Houzz, Facebook).

This gives your contractor a future benefit and increases their online reputation. The whole process might take thirty minutes—certainly a small token of appreciation for a job well done!

■ ■ ■

Chapter Recap
- Expect a prompt response to warranty items and issues.
- Conduct a wrap-up meeting.
- Provide a contractor review.

We're Here to Help,
It's What We Do!

I hope you've enjoyed this book on experiencing a painless remodel via the CRATE Way. And I truly mean that word: *experience*. After all, if you set your project up correctly, not only should you expect a fantastic finished product, but you should also have had a pleasurable experience along the way. It took quite a while to distill all this information, but I hope it benefits many of you in your remodel adventure.

We created kitchen & bath CRATE back in 2012. Since then we've had the honor of remodeling more than one thousand rooms for fantastic clients throughout Northern California.

If we can assist you in any way, either with a kitchenCRATE or bathCRATE or with a project you're managing on your own, please don't hesitate to reach out to me at 888-995-7996.

As always, *kbcrate.com* has hundreds of project profiles and helpful resources for you as you embark on your remodel journey.

Cheers!

NOTES:

Start planning!